THE ART OF STILLNESS

Kristin Dewane

This book is dedicated to my Dad.
Thanks for being such a great
example of my heavenly Father and a
nice earthly Dad too.

CHAPTER ONE

"Be still, and know that I am God; I will be exalted among the nations, I will be exalted in the earth. The Lord almighty is with us; the God of Jacob is our fortress."
Psalm 46:10&11

What does that verse mean exactly? The dictionary definition of stillness (as I am using it in this book) is : deep silence and calm. Just typing those words actually makes me feel a little calmer. Similar to when you make yourself take a deep breath, or close your eyes and quiet your mind at the end of a long day. Or maybe you don't know what that's like. Maybe you go at life full tilt until you crash in bed and need warm milk or a double shot of vodka to fall asleep. How's that workin' for ya?

That good, huh? That's what I thought. Yeah, I just read your mind. You're on a treadmill trying to get that carrot hanging just out of reach. You're never gonna get it, my friend. Tomorrow will be no different from today. Do you want it to be different? Do you want to know what it's like to crunch that carrot between your teeth? The one you've been chasing all your life, wondering how it will taste? Read the verse again. Go on, do it. It's short. It says we need to calm ourselves and in deep silence **know** that he is our God. That he **will** be exalted, even if it seems like he is not even a consideration for most of us much of the time. And that he **is** our fortress, even if it feels like we are left twisting in the wind. Feelings are not truths. Feelings are manipulated by the words of our friends and blood sugar and the state of our hormones. Feelings are not to be trusted. We need real truth, solid, dependable, un-fluctuating truth.

This is where the Bible comes in handy. Let's add Isaiah 30:15 to our deliberations. "In repentance and rest is your salvation, in quietness and trust is your strength, but you would have none of it."

Do you need strength? According to this verse, stillness and trust is the answer to getting strength. Go back and read the first verse again. Be calm, and know your God. Know that he will be exalted. This is where the trust comes in. You can't really be still unless you have trust. Think about it. If you were on a plane going down over the ocean, could you be still? What if the pilot was talking to you over the intercom, assuring you that it was going to be fine. Let's say you knew the pilot, he or she was someone you knew to be very competent and trustworthy. Now the stillness comes a little easier. In order to be still, to have calm in the deep silence, you have to trust something. Even if you don't think you are a trusting person. You are trusting that the food you recently consumed was not poisoned. You are trusting that your neighbor who is currently out on his riding lawn mower won't drive through your front window. You are trusting in gravity, that you won't fly off the world. You are trusting in me enough to be willing to read these words even though I could be a total nut-job. See, lots of trust going on.

Now extend that trust to the creator of the universe. He is the author of gravity, and the one who made the raw ingredients for the food you ate. He made your neighbor into the good guy that he is. And even if you doubt it sometimes, because life does not go your way all the time, he *is* trustworthy. And being still before him, and trusting in him, is the only way to be strong. The only way to have peace in a crazy world that is doing it's best to run you ragged and rob you of the very thing you need.

Stillness.

If you are one of those super strong people who hardly ever doubt and rarely feel weak or tired or scared then you don't need this. At least not now. Probably someday, because you are not superhuman. But for now I wonder why you are even reading this. Admit you will "have none of it". You are perfectly happy to run until you crash. So go help some old lady across the street and leave this book for the people who really need it. Ordinary people, weary people, restless and secretly frightened people.

People like me.

I have been in a low place lately. Really low, like having trouble getting out of bed low. Maybe that never happens to you. Maybe you wake up all sunshine and unicorns and make all the not-morning people growl at you over their coffee cups. Maybe your life is exactly how you want it to be. If that is so then put down this book and thank God and go do something else. Just please don't tell me about it. Especially if it's morning.

But maybe you have days like mine, when you want to just stay under the covers and hide from life. Maybe you've had months like mine, or even years. I am writing this book for you. And hopefully, it will help me too.

You see I didn't want to write this book. Just like I didn't want to get up this morning. I argued with God about it. My silent conversation went something like this:

"Why should I get up? My kids are older. I don't have to feed anyone or change diapers or pack a lunch. My hubby has long since got up and gone to work and he won't care. In fact, if I lie here all day and never get up I don't think anyone will miss me or even notice. I am a nothing, a no one." That's quite the pity party isn't it? But I wasn't talking to myself. I invited God to my party, even though there was no cake and no balloons and certainly no presents, other than my tears. But my father God, showing his usual infinite patience with me and my whining, spoke to me. Just three little words.

"I need you."

What? God needed me? I had to be imagining it. But I am very familiar with recognizing God's voice and I knew I would not say those words to myself. Did I jump out of bed and shout hooray? God just spoke to me! The Master of the Universe and Author of all good things responded to my self-pity session! I should have thanked him or praised him or something. No, being the stubborn person I am I just continued to argue with him about it.

"You can't need me. You're God. You don't need anyone, least of all me."

But God doesn't argue. He doesn't waste time trying

to convince me. He speaks straight to the heart, kindly, because he knows I am sensitive, but with the directness I need. He reminds me why he made man in the first place. And this is something I have already learned. But apparently, he wants me to share it with you. He *needs* me to, because you need to hear it. So he gives me the choice to get up and obey him, or continue to lay there wallowing in self-castigation. God is a gentleman, and he always gives a choice, never forcing us to do what he wants. But I know him, and I know what he wants me to do is always for my own good. That's where trust comes in.

I haul my hiney out of bed.

I used to hate the creation story. Not the part where God makes the sky and the stars and the trees, that is a beautiful picture of my very creative God. What I disliked was the part where he makes Adam first.

Because I am a female.

I wanted to be God's first human creation, not his afterthought. Not the thing made because no animal was a suitable companion. And telling me I was made to be some guy's "helpmeet" did not lessen the sting *at all.* I wanted to be *God's* companion, his best creation, his first choice. And no amount of Bible study or church teaching or patronizing pats on the head could change my feelings.

You, dear reader, will quickly learn that I am a chronic questioner. But even though most people expect me to just accept things like a good little girl, God does not have a problem with questions. He is not afraid of questions, even ones about him. He can take it.

And he can answer them. As I pondered my questions and read the story again, something struck me.

The Bible says that both Adam *and Eve* were created in the image of God. So that means both man and woman, together, represent what God is like. Animals are not made in his image, therefore none of them would be right as a partner for Adam. *And God knew this.* He had to know, if he is omniscient. So why bother with the whole charade of parading the animals before Adam if he knew they wouldn't do? He did it for Adam, of course. Adam needed to know that Eve was his special partner, created by God to not only complete him, but to show the world what God is like. He is both male and female. Only together do we see all the attributes of God; provider, nurturer, protector, and creator of life.

So I am not an afterthought. God does not have afterthoughts. He is the great architect of the universe, and he had a plan all along. And you and I are part of it.

God tells stories for a reason. When I read the creation story, knowing what I know about God, I see another picture emerge. God is in heaven, and Jesus is with him. They create angels. Angels to me are like the animals of heaven. Just as there are different orders of animals, with different levels of intelligence and emotions, so there are different orders of angels (this is all in the bible). And angels are great, except those stupid rebellious ones, but they are not enough. God wants siblings for his son. His son wants a bride. What to do?

This is where we come in. We are not Angels: Mark II. No, we are what was intended all along. Like Eve, we are made to be the companion Jesus desires. We were born because we *were needed*. No matter what anyone has ever said to you, or anything you have told yourself, **you are needed**. God needed me to tell you this, and you needed to hear it.

So get up.

The creation story is right at the beginning of the bible, Genesis chapter 1 & 2.

Let's go back to my story about the pilot and the soon-to-be-crashing plane. I mentioned how it would help your ability to be still and trust if you knew the pilot personally. That makes sense right? And just "knowing about" the pilot like you "know about" the Queen of England or your favorite celebrity is not the same as "knowing" someone like you know your best friend or significant other. You know (and hopefully trust) your best friend because you have spent a significant amount of time with them, you have shared secrets, you have gone through crisis together, you have shared joys and sorrows. You may get an autograph from a celebrity and read about them in a magazine while waiting in the doctors' office, but they are only as trustworthy to you as others who really know them have said they are. Who would you trust with your life if you had to choose, the Queen of England or your bestie? It's a no-brainer right, even though the Queen is probably pretty cool.

It is the same with God. Most of us know about him

like we know about the Queen. We have read books, listened to sermons, and sang songs. We have maybe even talked about him or discussed him on social media or put a bumper sticker about him on our cars. We have given him our money and our time. But we only know him second-hand. We haven't shared our secrets with him, or invited him on our vacations or cried on his shoulder. Yet we claim to trust him. But we don't really trust him to the level of letting him pilot our crashing plane without panicking. We aren't still, knowing he is our God. We don't want to see him exalted, because that would mean putting ourselves down below him. We know that's where we belong, but to actually do it is bone-jarringly terrifying.

Because we don't know him. We can't be still. We won't get off the treadmill because that's all we know, and it seems to be working. Or does it? Aren't you tired? In need of strength to get through the day? If I took away your coffee, your internet, your chocolate, or even your freedom, would you still be okay? Is God alone enough for you?

Honest moment here. I'll go first. I don't feel like God is enough. There, I've said it. And no lightning has struck me down. I know in my head he is enough, I sing it, preach it, say it to myself. But I don't know if I really believe it. Did you know that what you claim to believe is often not what you really believe? Your actions will tell you what you really believe. We fool ourselves and busy ourselves with religious ritual (treadmills) and are afraid to stop because deep down we know that all is not right. We are clutching our souls so tight if we let go we are afraid of bleeding out. We are desperate to make sure we always get what we want. We fill ourselves with junk food, junk media, junk relationships. Yet we are unsatisfied.

Spoiler alert: all those times you didn't let God in to your moments, and hid from him, he was there anyway. Just waiting. Longing for you to let him in so he can comfort you. That's not so scary, is it? And that will continue until you die. He will never give up on you, or get tired of waiting. That I do believe. But we are breaking his heart by making him wait.

I know that God is enough. I just don't truly believe it, or I would act like it. But that can change. That I also believe. I just need to know him better, to move him from the status of the Queen to my very best friend.

I just need to figure out *how*.

And I believe God will show us together.

CHAPTER TWO

"For God so loved the world that he gave his one and only son, that whoever believes in him shall not perish but have eternal life. For God did not send his son into the world to condemn the world, but to save the world through him."
John 3:16&17

You're up. Good for you. Have you had coffee or gotten dressed or showered or whatever it takes to wake yourself up? Maybe all three? Alright, go you!

Now we get to figure out what God needs you for. And to do that we need to be able to hear his voice. Maybe you're at the place in your walk with Jesus that you can just cock your head and instantly hear what he wants to say. Maybe you're more normal, like me for instance. Or maybe you don't even know what I mean by a "walk with Jesus" and you're ready to throw this stupid book down because I am annoying you with weird phrases. To walk with Jesus just means to take him with you as you go through life. Basically it's like getting to know anyone, the more you spend time with them, the better you know them. Of course you can read the Bible and various devotions and books (like this one, good choice by the way) and learn about God that way. But just like with a person you might be dating or working with or living with, speaking face to face is always imperative. And I don't mean Skype or Snap chat or any other of those technological breakthroughs that have kept us more connected on the surface but further from the heart than ever before. I mean actual soul to soul, one open living being to another.

So here's what we're gonna do. We're going to drop this book and go find a quiet place and shut everything off. No T.V., no music, no phones or internet of any kind. And no other person either. Just you and God. One on one. Mano e' mano. At least just try and do absolutely nothing but be still in his presence, for five whole minutes. Think you can do that? Doesn't sound too hard? Okay, I will see you back here in five minutes.

Alright, are you back? How did it go? I am going to ignore all the cheater cheater pumpkin eaters who didn't actually do it (It's not too late you know if you go now) and guess how it went with the rest of you. I am pretty confident in saying it did not go well. If you were anything like me you had trouble sitting still that long. Your mind went to a thousand places even though you kept trying to haul it back to just being open to God. You found yourself reviewing last night's movie, or thinking about your grocery list or the upcoming soccer game. Or you felt silly and a little guilty sitting there doing nothing. What are you trying to accomplish anyway?

Here's the deal. We don't know how to be still anymore. We don't value stillness. When was the last time you just sat and watched a sunset or listened to the rain? Watched the wind sway the trees? Listened to the sound of silence? *Without looking at your phone or taking a selfie.* Generations before us knew how to relax and enjoy the world God made but that skill has been lost to the perils of modern technology and our super fast, jam-packed lifestyles. If just five little minutes of stillness is too much, what does that say about us?

And this is why we don't know God. We know *about* him. We know facts and can quote verses and can get in people's faces with our opinions about him. But we haven't spent time with him, haven't exposed our souls to his searching gaze, and haven't wanted to gaze back. But we have to. I for one am sick of living without it. I am sick of busyness and shallowness and emptiness. And besides, he needs me.

I just might need him too.

Here's the real problem with being still. We don't like it. If we stay busy we not only feel productive but we have a real good excuse to not be still. If we are still we may have to lift the tarp that's covering our mound of rottenness. You know what I mean. That secret place where we hide all our failings, our faults, our sin. No one wants to look at it. It's better to pretend it's not there. We definitely don't want God poking his nose in there.

Go ahead, take a peek. Not pretty, is it? You are probably irritated with me for even bringing it up. You're thinking that you have something better to do right now than read this book.

Take courage, my friend. We are in this together. So stay with me.

I am now going back to the story of Adam and Eve. After they ate the forbidden fruit the bible tells us that they were ashamed and hid from God. But God came looking for them. I always questioned this part of the story too. God came down to walk with them in the garden and he couldn't find them? This is *God* we're talking about. He created the garden and the people in it yet not only does he call out, "Where are you?" but Adam and Eve actually think they can hide from him. It's a bit like playing hide and seek with the kid who hides behind the curtains and the bottom of his legs stick out. It's ridiculous.

But God always has a reason. And in this story he begins to show us his nature. He wants to be with his creation. Even after they have betrayed him. He knows what they did, and instead of just smacking them down the minute they eat the fruit, he waits. He lets them try to hide, and try to make clothes for themselves. Then he calls to them. This is his love in action.

I have a news flash for you. God knows what's under the tarp. He knows everything you have ever done. **He is God.**

But he waits for you to show him. He calls to you, giving you the chance to come clean. Like Adam and Eve we stupidly think if we don't spend time with him he won't see, he won't know. So we get busy trying to make ourselves clothes to cover our nakedness. And we ignore the smelly pile under the tarp and hope it will go away.

But God himself made clothes for Adam and Eve. He killed animals, some of his own beautiful creation, to cover them. And we have it even better. We live in the days after Jesus came and died, so we don't need to have any animals killed to clothe us. God allowed his own son to die. His blood covers us, giving us the clean white robes to wear.

So lift the tarp and let him wipe it clean. Not even a stain or whiff will remain. Nothing required except the acknowledgment that it is there and needs his cleansing touch.

Or keep living with it. Your choice. He will not force you to reveal it. But he will keep patiently calling, "Where are you?"

What are you waiting for?

Did you know that when you leave God waiting you make the devil dance? He loves it. And this is Lucifer we are talking about. The enemy of your soul, the one responsible for inciting mankind to do every dirty, horrible thing to each other throughout all of history. Do you want him to dance, to be so pleased with you that his pointy clawed feet do a spontaneous jig?

I am not trying to guilt you into spending time with God. I am letting you know that letting guilt keep you from him is the thing Satan wants most. He doesn't just want you to sin. He has *tons* of people doing that stuff for him. He wants to keep you from having a meaningful relationship with God, or to at least interrupt the one you are currently enjoying. That is his ultimate goal. Because your sin is covered. All you have to do is confess it, even to just be sorry in the slightest, and the blood of Jesus is there instantly. The bible says your sins are removed "as far as the east is from the west". Do you understand what that means? We live on a globe, so if you start traveling east looking for the west you will never get there. As long as you are going east, there will always be more east in front of you. Get it? The devil can chase you all around the globe with condemnation, **but he can never reach you.**

But when you choose to avoid God because you think your sin makes you unacceptable, you let the devil catch you. You agree with his words of condemnation. Don't agree with the devil about anything! He is a liar, and the father of lies. He is a loser who has taken it badly. He is responsible (through others) for those bad things that happened to you, not God. He desperately wants to keep you from God, so that you never learn how awesome God is. He emphatically doesn't want you to grow strong in Christ, so you will be able to resist his wiles. And he most definitely (and I am running out of strong adverbs) doesn't want you helping others with what you learn. The Rolling Stones were right; hustlin' you is the nature of his game. He wants you to stay in bed.

Don't let him. I am praying for you (and myself) right

now, that we will recognize his tactics and not let his lies stay in our minds and hearts. Father God, give us the power to resist the devil, and he will flee from us. I want him not to dance, but to flee! Keep the eyes of our hearts open to you God and the truth of who you are. Jesus loves me, this I know. For the bible tells me so. People like me to him belong. We are weak, but he is strong. Yes, Jesus loves me.

Yes, Jesus loves me.

Yes, Jesus loves me.

I am telling myself so.

"As far as the east is from the west, so far has he removed our transgressions from us." Psalm 103:12

CHAPTER THREE

"For I know the plans I have for you, declares The Lord, plans to prosper you and not to harm you, plans to give you a hope and a future. Then you will call on me and pray to me, and I will listen to you. You will seek me and find me when you seek me with all your heart."
Jeremiah 29:11&12

Perhaps you think it's easy for me to say these things to you because I can hear God's voice and seem to know a lot of bible stuff. Trust me, it wasn't always that way. Everyone has a beginning when they tell their story of faith and I have mine.

I was raised in a Christian home. My grandfather was a pastor. My mother was involved in Bible studies, prayer groups, and women's ministries all of my life. She always seemed to have it all together and I often wondered how she got that way and why I wasn't like her. I felt I was somehow unable to find her way or the faith of my many other role models because I was sub-standard. God didn't speak to me because he knew I wasn't as good as those others. Therefore I should just give up.

I remember talking to my Mom about my struggles one day. She told me I would find God when I sought after him with my whole heart. I dutifully listened but after she left I wept bitterly. I really thought I *had* been seeking with my whole heart. So now I was justified in believing I was never going to have her faith. My life would always be devoid of God's voice and favor.

So I tried to fill that void with other things. I dove into the typical pleasures the world had to offer; parties, boys, friends, food, television. I often wiggled my toes in the pool of my own imagination, where I could pretend life was how I wanted it and everyone treated me how I wanted to be treated. I think that's why I liked writing so much. I could make the world how I wanted it to be. Even if it wasn't real.

But somewhere in the back of my mind was the constant niggling feeling that I hadn't really sought God with my whole heart. Sure I had put out feelers, and tried to copy what others were doing. But had I ever put aside everything I wanted, given over complete control, and wanted to know him no matter the price? The honest answer was no. But like the tarp of stuff you don't want to peek under, I avoided the thoughts whenever they came. Usually when I was quiet and alone. God kept gently poking me on the back of my shoulder, waiting for me to turn and see him there.

I used to wear a jean jacket with a lot of buttons on it. A professor who was generously helping me with my writing gave me a button to add to my collection. It said something about adding "mission" to your life. It was suppose to be an advertisement for a missionary organization. I didn't really want to wear it, but I didn't want to offend her. So it went on the jacket with the others, most of which were quirky sayings or fan paraphernalia. One night I was standing in line at a fast food counter and some guy asked me about that particular button. I gave some vague reply about how everyone should have a mission in life, and not just float through it. But I realized suddenly that I didn't have a mission. I was a floater. What was my mission, my purpose? To make sure I didn't miss the next episode of "Full House"? To not wear the same outfit to the next party? To not embarrass myself in front of the cute guy who asked me about my button? What kind of lame purposes were those? I knew then I needed to stop playing around and find a real one.

Not long after that night I went home and threw out everything I thought was distracting me from finding God. I started going to a different church from where my family went. I determined to find God my own way, instead of trying to make myself like those around me. I went at it with my whole heart.

Now, that doesn't mean I immediately heard a voice booming from the sky saying, "Well done." I didn't. Building a relationship with God is the same as building one with a person. Remember we are made like him, so what works for people also works with God. It takes time and commitment. And there were definitely times I got off track, sat down and pouted, or got angry or discouraged and turned my back for a time. But there are two things I can say with certainty. God never gave up on me. And I have never been sorry I chose him.

Let me be clear. This book is not written to be your road map to God. There are no "Ten steps to knowing God" or "Five ways to conquer sin" that actually work. Wanting to hear God's voice and really know him is a life-altering decision you will have to make daily. It's a lot like dieting; you can't just eat kumquats and yogurt for a month and expect to stay skinny for life. You have to change your lifestyle.

Actually all you have to do is chose him every day. He does the rest. Really, he does. Following God and hearing his voice is not hard to grasp, but it can be challenging to maintain. The devil will fight you all the way. But the good news is your champion Jesus already whipped his red-tailed butt. So you've got this.

I remember once a friend of mine said he had to get rid of some sin before he could commit to meeting in a group setting. The group wanted to have more accountability and support with their struggles. I sympathized with his desire to come to the group without carrying that shame, but I hope you can see the ridiculousness of his attitude. It would be like an alcoholic saying he had to be free of his addiction before he could go to an AA meeting. The point of the group was that we *couldn't* get rid of our sin ourselves. Only God can do it in us, and we need each other to help us let it go. I wish he knew that we all had sin. And I wish he had gone to the group, because to my knowledge he never did.

God does not expect you to rid yourself of your sin before you approach him. In fact, he knows you can't. That's why Jesus died, people! To try to do it ourselves is to slap him in the face or maybe just kiss him like Judas and tell him we don't need him. Think about it.

No really, stop and think about it. Jesus died for all sin, for everything, once and for all. To think we could or should do something to help him get rid of our sin is hypocritical and insulting. He died hard enough for you. Accept it.

Now we can move on. Because he does want us to

partner with him. It's a relationship, not a possession. He won't stop your hand from reaching out to take that thing that causes your downfall. But he will absolutely help you resist if you ask him to. And he will totally forgive you when you fail.

Every time.

Over and over.

He doesn't get sick of us and our stupidity even when we are sick of ourselves. That's what makes him so wonderful.

So are you sick of yourself? Tired of floating along with no purpose? Had enough of empty religious steps that just walk you in circles?

Then keep reading, and keep choosing.

My Mom is forever giving me books to read. She loves books, and so do I, but many of the ones she has given me over the years have not been what I would have chosen myself. In many ways that's a good thing, because it makes me stretch my narrow reading boundaries and often God uses the very ones I initially sneer at to teach me things I wouldn't have otherwise learned as easily. I normally tend to learn things the hard way, which by now probably doesn't shock you. My stubbornness has forced me onto my face in the dirt many times. But on occasion it has helped me.

I will explain.

Once I received a book to read. I don't remember the name of the book, or the author, or even the cover illustration. I don't even know for sure who loaned it to me, but I highly suspect it was my Mom. The book was almost certainly non-fiction and auto-biographical. It was meant to be a teaching book, a devotional of sorts. But I also fail to recall much about the actual contents of the book. There was just one scene out of the whole book that affected me so strongly that it literally changed my life. And that's the one thing I'll never forget.

In the scene the author of the book was at some sort of religious conference. I think he might have been a speaker or a pastor or something like that. He talked about how much he was enjoying the conference, and being with all the people. But then he reached a point where he had enough. He didn't want to speak anymore or listen to another teaching or sing another song or talk to another person. He needed, *wanted,* to get away to be alone with his God. He described it as "his heart pounding in anticipation" of communing alone with his Lord. He loved being with God that much. Even though he had all the friends and all the religious activity he could want. It was not what satisfied him.

I remember a feeling of disbelief. This guy is really admitting his heart pounds for God like he was a love-sick school boy? Is that even possible? I think he even talked about finding a closet or store-room or something in order to be alone. Here was this popular guy who had people who hung on his every word and wanted to be around him and he goes off to a closet to be with God?

What would that be like? I wondered.

I thought it would be awesome.

I wanted it.

I could just imagine having that kind of desire for God, someone who was always there for me, who could make me feel giddy and excited and loved when I needed it. But it seemed like a far-off dream. I was just an ordinary small town housewife and not a pastor and author. I hadn't done any of the things the man in the book had done in his life.

But this is where my stubbornness came in to save me from giving up. If God loved us all equally, and I had to believe he did, then he can also **be loved** by us all equally. It didn't matter if I was a maid or a president, I could have that same passion for God. I **would** have it!

I determined in my own stubborn way to keep reaching for God until I felt that same heart pounding desire to be alone with him. I can't honestly say I achieved my goal. But I have made significant progress. I can hear his voice fairly easily and when I haven't spent any time with him in awhile I notice that I get very anxious and depressed and crabby. I need him. And I believe the heart-pounding is on it's way. I will keep believing until I die.

I'm stubborn that way.

Thanks Mom for the book.

CHAPTER FOUR

"You have heard that it was said, 'Love your neighbor and hate your enemy.' But I tell you, love your enemies and pray for those who persecute you, that you may be children of your Father in heaven. He causes his sun to rise on the evil and the good, and sends rain on the righteous and the unrighteous. If you love those who love you, what reward will you get? Are not even the tax collectors doing that?"
Matthew 5:43-46

Let me ask you a question. If you are one of the millions of people who go to a church of some kind every week or so, why do you go? Stop and think before you answer. Is it because you think (or have been taught) that it's the right thing to do? Or you really like a good sermon? Or you like to sing somewhere other than the shower? Do you go because you like to socialize or hang out with your friends? Or because people expect you to be there?

There is nothing wrong with agreeing with any of those answers. But they are not good enough for me.

I was raised in church. After I got married my husband and I attended many different churches, looking for the right fit. The problem was we didn't really fit anywhere. Okay, if I'm being honest, the problem was me. I hate getting dressed up. I hate small talk. And I absolutely hate being fake. To me, church involved all of those hateful things. Occasionally I would hear a sermon that made it worthwhile, or would have an encounter with God during the worship. But mostly I just marked my time and got through it. This is what a good Christian did, so I did it. But of course, secretly in my heart, I questioned it.

I remember the day the realization came to me; *there is no law against staying home.* I might be criticized, publicly snubbed, and gossiped about, but no one could arrest me or force me to attend a Sunday service. I would not be dragged there and chained to a pew. The freedom I felt at that moment was incredible.

I like my freedom. As a child I refused to go to summer camp like my siblings. Partly because I was shy, but mostly because I couldn't stand the idea of being told when to get up, when to eat, and when to make a macaroni necklace. This was *my* summer and nobody was going to mess with it.

It is one of the reasons that I home schooled my kids. I wanted to give them a freedom in their studies that I lacked with my public school education. And it's a reason I could never live in a gated community where I would be told how many flower beds to have and what color to paint my garage. I would go with a fuchsia color scheme (maybe with a mural of dogs playing poker) and plant a huge beds of dandelions just to be different. Yeah, I might be a little rebellious.

Of course this is why I don't fit in well at church. I can fake it for awhile, but why? Why try to be like everyone else if I don't have to? I wasn't any closer to knowing God or hearing his voice. In fact, I had so many other voices in my head telling me how to live and what to believe that I couldn't even hear myself. But God still kept pursuing me, and he used my discontent with the status quo to drive me into the wilderness.

When I speak of "the wilderness" I don't mean I went camping. The phrase is more metaphorical. Though if temporarily hiding from civilization in a cave somewhere was what it would have taken, I would have done it. And I really, really adore indoor plumbing.

Basically I took a hiatus from church and all the outward religious trappings that go with it. A lot of my more religious friends and family kind of freaked out. Just like a lot of readers are freaking out right now. But wait, there's more. I even stopped reading my Bible for awhile.

On purpose.

Some people have headed to the nearest fireplace to burn this book of blasphemy. And that might be tough if they are reading the kindle version. But for those of you who are still with me I will explain why.

I had to get all the voices out of my head. I don't mean actual audible voices, so quit panicking. I mean I had to be able to approach God by myself, not on the coattails of my family heritage, or on the basis of my church membership. I needed to know the real Jesus, not the beautiful holy-looking guy from the paintings, or the man from all the Bible studies I had completed that filled my head with knowledge (often contradictory) about who he was and what he wanted from me. I wanted to be able to read the Bible and not hear the voices of all the preachers who used those verses for their sermons and sometimes for their own benefit. I had to go on a religious cleanse.

It felt good.

Jesus himself was sent into the wilderness by the Spirit of God before he did any miracles or preached any sermons. I imagine it was preparation for all that he was about to do. But according to the Bible, the devil tempted him there. And in any wilderness experience you will be tempted too. Without all the "voices" keeping you on the straight and narrow you will find out how badly you really want to know God. Did I need the shame my pastor might bring on me to keep me from sinning? Did I need all the people watching what I was wearing and how much I put in the offering plate to coerce me into doing right? Or could my love of God and his love for me be enough?

I remember telling one concerned friend that if I needed the fence to keep me in the pasture then I was not really in it with all my heart. And I wanted to be there with all my heart. That's the only way I would truly find him. The *real* him.

Do you want him? Because he wants you, and he will keep you from falling in the wilderness if you ask him to. So don't be afraid. It's like any undertaking, you just need to be prepared.

So let's get packed.

For the record, I am not advocating ditching the Bible and your church (if you have one) and going to a remote cave and contemplating your navel. If your navel looks like mine that would not only be weird but also depressing. I just needed to do those things in order to stop trying to fit in and please everyone. Just like I had to throw away a bunch of "worldly" things when I decided to seek after God with my whole heart. It wasn't that those things were bad in themselves, they were just distractions that made it harder to seek him. And later those distractions came in a religious form. Until I was able to be strong enough in my faith to believe on my own, I had to get away from the busyness and the people pleasing and the religious knowledge that took God's place in my life.

Unfortunately the church today is really good at having everyone look like the supermodels of the religious world. Most people, especially if you are a woman, look at the pictures of models and instantly feel inadequate. We may know in our head that they look that way because of make-up artists and Botox and special lighting. We may tell ourselves that it isn't normal or even healthy to be so skinny and have teeth that white. But we still suddenly either want to run around the block three times and eat only kale and spinach smoothies or dive into a bag of cheese puffs and crawl out the other end. Having those images in our faces all the time, even when we know they are false, does something terrible to our self-esteem.

When we go to church on Sunday and see everyone dressed to kill, chatting comfortably in their cliques, always smiling and looking well, we experience the same feelings of inadequacy. Although we know in our heads that those people must still sometimes get baby spit up on their shirts and have bad hair days, we still feel like the orphan child nobody wants. Maybe they secretly struggle with stuff like us, and occasionally cry themselves to sleep like us, but our emotions over-ride our brains and we just want to be like them. Somewhere there has to be a class that can teach us how to liposuction our problems away and whiten our image like our teeth. Sadly, there is probably a preacher out there who will sell you a book about it for $19.95. Plus shipping and handling.

Did you know that Jesus did not dress to kill? And his teeth were very likely not white? He did not have a clique of religious teachers that he hung around with. Jesus befriended the lowlifes of his day. He talked to tax collectors (considered the scum of the earth back then), fishermen (nobodies), women (a big no-no) and even prostitutes (yikes). The only people he was ever angry and harsh with were the religious leaders of the day, the ones who thought they were something special. The religious super models. Read the gospels and you will see what I mean. He calls them hypocrites, snakes, sons of hell, and white-washed tombs. He wasn't subtle. He was serious about how those who claimed to represent God should be living. He said it is the things of the heart, the inside of a man, not his outer image, that matters. He spoke hard, loved hard, and died hard. He wasn't the Jesus of the big blue eyes and spotless robe and halo we see in paintings. He was a real man, who hurt and cried and bled and died.

And that Jesus was the one I needed to know.

The gospels are Matthew, Mark, Luke, and John. They are right at the beginning of the New Testament and the best place to start reading your bible. They tell the story of Jesus' life and death from four different perspectives.

CHAPTER FIVE

"Like water spilled on the ground, which cannot be recovered, so we must die. But that is not what God desires; rather he devises ways so that a banished person does not remain banished from him."
2nd Samuel 14:14

I have listened to a lot of sermons in my time. Yes, that means I've been around awhile. But let's stick to the point. I have been taught a lot of things, attended a lot of bible studies and prayer meetings and retreats. And few things bother me more than spending my valuable time listening to motivational speeches or flowery prose or fire and brimstone warnings that don't really pertain to my life. Don't preach at me about God, tell me how to reach him! Tell me why I can't seem to do it myself. Answer my questions about faith that everyone around me seems to think are blasphemous. How does what you're saying (and in many cases what I'm paying you to say) have anything to do with my life RIGHT NOW.

Am I the only one who ever felt this way? Most of the time I don't reveal my inner turmoil because that would mean removing the mask I wear that makes me look like everyone else. And I have learned the hard way that people don't like questions like mine. They get very uncomfortable.

Once I was put in charge of a Bible study. The poor fools didn't know what they were doing. The very first night I asked everyone to share a story from a time in their life when they felt God had let them down. They looked at me like I should be burned at the stake. They all claimed to have never been let down by God. And I was told to keep the study to just Bible knowledge and no personal stuff after that.

Of course I left there thinking something was terribly wrong with me. I was the only one who ever doubted God. I was a horrible Christian. So what could I do now? My choices were to go back to faking it, or to just not go back. Well if you read the last chapter you know what I eventually did.

If you have ever felt let down by God I want you to know you are not alone. And he doesn't hate you for your doubts. I don't hate you for your doubts. We could probably be friends. I am writing this book because he wants me to share my story and encourage those who feel let down and alone. Or those who are just tired of listening to empty words repeated over and over every week. Tired of faking it.

I could write you a poetic devotional about God's grace and love and quote scriptures and give prophetic words. Really I could. I am a writer, I have done all those things in the past. But I am going to be real and blunt and try to give you something that pertains to your life today. And not because I'm such a nice person or because I have a burning desire to write this book. No, I am writing this because God asked me to. Because he loves you and wants to help you, right here, right now. He wants you to find him, and he wants to show you how.

How's that for poetry?

So let's review. We've established that God made you because he needs you. He desires you. You, as a human made in his image, and you as an individual, unique and special, unlike anyone else in the world. No one else can do the things he has planned for you to do, or fulfill his heart's desire as you can. The Bible says he knit you together in your mother's womb. You are no accident, no matter what anyone may have told you. But you have to choose to believe it. He waits patiently for you to grab hold of this concept, and invite him to walk with you.

I believe the creation story is another proof of this idea. He didn't make the woman second because she was a secondary thought. God carefully plans everything, and he doesn't have secondary thoughts. Consider again the idea I presented earlier: God creates angels, his first creations, and pretty cool ones at that. But when presented to his son, they prove to be not meeting the mark as companions. Jesus wants someone made to be like him in a way that completes him. So God makes man. **In his own**

image. Angels were like the animals, awesome and powerful and with some level of personality, but not like God. WE, humans, are made like God. We are the only thing he created in his image.

Eve was not forced to be Adam's bride. She could have walked away. And we are not forced into a relationship with God. He made us with the ability to choose, because he wanted to be chosen. That makes sense, doesn't it? None of us would really want a robot spouse. We all want our partner to *want* us. The robot can do the chores around the house and will always act in the way it is programmed but it can't love you. And we as humans want to be loved. And we are made like God, so he wants to be loved too.

Of course this is just my own idea. There is no scripture story of God and his pet angels to corroborate it. But it makes sense to me, and it gives me another reason, as a woman, to view the creation story as something beautiful instead of derogatory. And keep in mind most of the old testament is symbolic, prophetic, or allegorical for things happening today. Those are big words, I know. You can look them up, but it just means that the purpose of the bible is to teach us about who God is and what he wants from us. It gives us a purpose. And everyone needs that.

I know I am repeating things here but they are important enough to be repeated. I want you to get this good. God made us and gave us our freedom, knowing we would turn away. We sold ourselves to Satan, but God was prepared to pay a great price to gain us back. That is love and desire right there. God made you, he wants you, he needs you, he loves you. And he wants to be needed and loved in return.

Make it personal: God made me. God wants me. God needs me. God loves me.

That's a very simple but profound truth.

Now that you know God needs you, what do you do with that information? If you have continued to read this then you haven't decided to just say "I don't care" and walk away. Do you know that you have already made him happy just by doing that? It is a huge step, and before you start to get scared about that information, just stop and reflect on the fact that you have just made God happy. The Maker of the universe, the King of kings, the Lord of lords, your Creator, can be made happy just by you not rejecting him. Don't let go of that amazing thought. You have made God smile. That should make you smile! And it can be enough for now. Just spend a few minutes, hours, or even days basking in his happiness.

Come back here when you are ready to continue.

Ready already? Most of you haven't done what I asked but that's okay. To continue to review: God needs you, you accept it. But you don't know how to know what exactly he needs. Reading the Bible is a good step, and I can add all the religious trappings too; church attendance, Bible studies, devotionals and small groups. But we come back to the same problem. God wants a relationship, he doesn't want to be the object of a dissertation or the subject of a Where's Waldo guessing game. You have to spend time with him to have a relationship with him.

So we are back to the problem of the impossible five minutes. How can we learn to spend time listening to God and building a relationship with him if we can't even give him five uninterrupted minutes of attention? We not only don't really want to because we are scared of him and what he will think of us, but we can't slow our minds and schedules down enough to focus even when we decide to be brave about it.

Wait.

Yes, we can. Yes, YOU can. He would not ask something of us that's impossible. Mark 10:27 states "What's impossible with man is possible with God." Jesus said that when his disciples complained about some rather hard teaching. He wanted them to love their fellow man (and their wives) and not have to be governed by a bunch of laws. But we all know that truly loving people selflessly is impossible. If you think you can do it then you haven't met the right people to challenge you yet, or your idea of love is messed up. I will be honest with you, most of the time I don't even *like* people, let alone love them. Yet Jesus says it is possible, but **with God**. John 15:5 says "Apart from him, we can do nothing." This is another good verse. And how about Philippians 4:13: "I can do all things through Christ who gives me strength."

We can't spend five minutes in God's presence on our own will power, but Jesus can do it through us. Our job is to *believe it's possible*.

Come believe with me.

CHAPTER SIX

"For this reason I kneel before the Father, from whom every family in heaven and on earth derives its name. I pray that out of his glorious riches he may strengthen you with power through his Spirit in your inner being, so that Christ may dwell in your hearts through faith. And I pray that you, being rooted and established in love, may have power together with all the Lord's people, to grasp how wide and long and high and deep is the love of Christ, and to know this love that surpasses knowledge - that you may be filled to the measure of all the fullness of God."
Ephesians 3:14-19

I believe I indicated how I feel about my freedom earlier. Hating camp and all that, remember? I like being able to do what I want with my time as much as possible. I like to make up my own additional rules to board games or scrap ones that I don't like. I tend to resist things like book clubs because I don't want someone else to choose my books for me. Does that make me a control freak or just a normal person? I guess it depends on who I'm asking. Not everyone will go to the extremes I do, but I don't think I am alone in being scared of a relationship with God because of control issues. I am being blunt and stating this openly as I promised. And keep in mind that I am including myself when I use the word "we".

We think God will take away our freedom. And it's scary. This is because we don't know him really, and trusting someone we don't know with our life is a frightening thing. It's much easier to trust in ourselves. We always look out for ourselves, don't we? Can God possibly love us more than we love ourselves? Even those times I think I hate myself deep down I really love me a lot. I hate things about myself because I love myself and want to be perfect because that's what I deserve, right? I don't want to control my environment because I dislike me. I want to protect me, and I go to great lengths to make sure I get what I want.

Think back to your childhood. Hopefully like me you had a normal one, and remembering it isn't a traumatic thing. If it is, I am sorry. Truly sorry. That's not what God had in mind for you, and part of why he wants a relationship with you now is to bring healing and wholeness into your life, even your past. So stay with me.

Now let's go back to our childhoods. Image one different from your own, maybe Leave it To Beaver's, if you have to. As long as it's a good childhood, one where you knew your parents loved you. Imagine it; it's a beautiful summer day. You have nothing you have to do, no responsibilities, other than breathing. You step out into the sunshine, feel the breeze on your face. Your friends call to you, or maybe you just head to your favorite treehouse with a book, or take a ride on your bike. Your thoughts are all about you, and what you will do. The whole day is in front of you. Endless possibilities, no worries. You know lunch will be ready for you, and supper too. The clothes you dirty up will get clean, almost as if by magic. You don't even think about it.

Now that's true freedom.

I think surrendering to God is something like that. Instead of feeling stifled and controlled, we would feel free, because our father would be taking care of us. He has the responsibility of getting us to grow up, and we get to just bask in the sunshine and trust in his magic.

That doesn't sound so scary, does it? We just need to know he loves us, and that he is a patient and loving father.

Still scared? Yeah, me too.

Maybe you and I can do this together. Will you (metaphorically speaking) hold my hand?

I will hold yours.

I promise.

Most of us trusted our parents to take care of us, or we were just so innocent that we believed in the magic of the never-empty fridge or un-ending pile of clean underwear. But when it comes to God, we are unfortunately not so trusting or innocent. This is the source of our fear. We think of God as the guy in heaven wearing the shirt with the word "fun" in a circle with a slash through it. Or the big scowling guy on the throne just waiting for a reason to blast us with a lightning bolt.

But let's look at the God of the Bible and think about him. He's the one who called to Adam and Eve in the garden in order to give them a chance to come clean even though he knew where they were, remember? And throughout the Old Testament he kept forgiving his people even though they rejected him time and time again. And how often have we dragged his name through the mud and expected (and received) forgiveness and understanding? And in the New Testament he was willing to live first as a carpenter and then as a homeless wanderer when he could have been born in a palace and been waited on his whole life. Think about it.

And then there is the story of the cross. There is no greater picture of how much he loved us than the fact that he died for us. You know he didn't have to redeem us, right? He could have given us up as a lost cause. And he didn't even have to suffer the way he did, or subject himself to the humiliation of being birthed in a stable and raised in a humble village. You might argue that he was fulfilling the prophecies in scripture but consider this; **he inspired the scriptures**. So basically he could have written it any way he wanted to. How about just appearing in the sky and pricking his finger on a poisoned spinning needle and dying? Or a nice quick death by beheading or something? All he needed to do to cover our sins was to die. Yet he chose to come at a point in history where he would have a hard life, and suffer and die in one of the most horrific and humiliating ways. Why? Why would he do that? He was not some sort of masochist. He did it that way so he could both understand our frailties and show the depth of his love. Do you get that? He did it for you!

Once I was having an argument with someone close to me. He was angry that things in his life were going wrong and he felt like God was not doing right by him. I can understand that thought. People think it all the time. Why does God let bad stuff happen to his kids? I will tackle this difficult question in more detail later but for now I will just tell you the same thing I told that person. Even if the only thing God ever does for you is the fact that he came and died, that's enough of a reason to serve him, and love him back.

End of discussion.

I once watched a movie that affected me profoundly. The actual movie itself (Battlefield Earth) was pretty terrible and I am not necessarily recommending it. But there was one scene in it that changed forever how I saw Jesus. In the scene the hero has finally got the villain at his mercy. He stands with his gun trained on the bad guy, ready to shoot. And you as the viewer are ready to see the villain, who was really quite despicable, get his just desserts. All you need is to hear the hero speak a sarcastic one-liner and then blast that jerk out of the picture. You can't wait for it to happen. But the hero surprises you. He doesn't kill the bad guy or even give him a satisfying telling-off. He just turns over his weapon and surrenders. It is then that the viewer wants to stand up and scream, "What are you doing, fool? Shoot him!"

You soon learn the reason the hero turns himself over to the one who humiliated and tortured him. He knows that if he kills him now he will indeed be free, but he also knows that staying temporarily under the power of the enemy is the best chance he has of freeing **all** of his people. He chooses his people over himself.

I became fascinated by that scene. It stayed in my mind for days, weeks even, making me want to re-watch a movie that was not a great watch the first time around. Because God used that scene to show me something about the character of Jesus that I hadn't fully grasped until that day.

I grew up in a Christian home so I was very familiar with the Easter story. I watched several movie and mini-series versions of it, including the very bloody "Passion of The Christ". But knowing the story and understanding the choices Jesus made for me are two very different things. I knew he had to die to cover the sins of the world but I never thought about the fact that Jesus was not the helpless lamb he appeared to be in the movies. He is the hero of the story and when he rises from the dead he gets his triumphant moment but even that is without much fanfare. He turns himself over to the bad guys over and over again. He is betrayed by a friend and arrested. He is beaten and accused of false things in front of those who should have been his champions. He is humiliated and treated as a side show in the king's palace when he had every right to usurp Herod and claim his throne. He is tormented and whipped nearly to death by pagans who are taking over the land of his people.

And at any time he could have stopped it.

Imagine yourself in his place. Could you have taken even the first words of accusation if you had the evidence in your hands to exonerated yourself? Could you let yourself be made fun of by worthless drunks when you could have silenced them with a word? Could you have allowed that whip to keep coming down on your abused flesh when you had the power to stand up and annihilate them? Could you have stayed on the cross and suffered hours of agony for a people that were at that moment laughing and reveling in your suffering?

I know I couldn't. Yet Jesus did it. And not because

he was some unfeeling all-powerful saint. His motivation, like the hero in the movie, was to save the people he loved.

That means you.

So the next time you feel unloved or forgotten, think of Jesus, allowing that whip to strike him again, because he was thinking of *you*. He resisted the rightful and tempting power right at his fingertips to save *you*.

That is a savior worthy of our surrender.

CHAPTER SEVEN

"We are therefore Christ's ambassadors, as though God were making his appeal through us. We implore you on Christ's behalf: Be reconciled to God. God made him who had no sin to be sin for us, so that in him we might become the righteousness of God." 2nd Corinthians 5:20

So we've established that God loves us. A lot. More than we deserve. And therein lies another problem. We want to deserve it. Nobody likes feeling like a charity case. It rankles, and our pride takes a hit. And if we don't deserve the love, we kind of doubt the quality of that love. We know we can't love someone well who doesn't deserve it. Let's be honest, we can't even tolerate them. And even though God is God, we still can't wrap our mind around the fact that he actually loves us undeserving schlubs.

This is something we have to believe by faith. You won't be able to wrap your head around it. It isn't logical. I can tell you that he wanted someone who was like him, more so than an angel, or that the Father wanted more children and Jesus wanted a bride. I can point out that he is omniscient, so he knew we would blow it big time. Yet he still chose to create us because he wanted someone who would choose him. I can quote a lot of scriptures about his love. But in the end you have to choose to believe it. Write those scriptures out and post them around your house if it helps. Memorize them and quote them to yourself when you have your moments of doubt.

And accept the fact that there is nothing you can do to deserve it. People have been trying for thousands of years and not succeeding. In fact, he doesn't want you to try to deserve it. That makes you like the religious leaders of old, the ones he called a brood of vipers and whitewashed tombs. True love is, by it's nature, undeserved and unearned. Think of every love story you've read or heard of, or experienced. Maybe things about that person helped you love them, but real solid love is the kind that occurs in sickness and in health, for better or for worse. That's the kind everyone wants, an undeserving kind of love that won't fade when things go south. The kind that is, at some point, a deliberate choice.

God chose to make us, and he chose to love us. Just believe it. The most poignant thing I can say to convince you is to quote Jesus from the cross. He was hanging there, bleeding and dying for people who had rejected him and spit on him and seemed to have forgotten that just days and weeks before he had been healing them and feeding them and teaching them about love. He was carrying, as if he was responsible for, every bad thing ever done to anyone. That's a huge weight that he experienced, even though he had done nothing wrong himself. He felt the pain of the concentration camp victim as they were stripped of their humanity, and the hatred of those who tormented them there. He felt the sting of the bullied, and the hidden pain of the bully himself who is secretly abused at home. He experienced the humiliation of the stripping of the innocence of the child, and the selfish lust that drives the abuser. Think of all the sin, of countless generations, crushing his soul in a flood of darkness and pain and grief. And he could have stopped it at any time.

Yet he hung there, with no one to comfort him, no one even appreciating what he was doing for them. Yet what did he say? "You'll get yours you miserable sods?" Or, "Someday I'll come back and show you what I can really do?" Maybe, "Please make it stop?" Those are the things we would say, or expect to hear if the story was the plot for a movie. But instead he said, "*Father forgive them, they don't know what they are doing.*"

He knows we are weak and yet thinks us worth dying for. So the deserving part has nothing to do with us and everything to do with him. We are his choice.

Now we get to choose him back.

Perhaps you have more questions. For example: How can God gives us his undivided attention and love when in reality he has to divide it between the other billions of people on the planet? Let me answer that with another example from your childhood. Like most children you probably spent part of your childhood believing in Santa Claus. And as you got older, the obvious questionable nature of his existence began to trouble you, unless you were one of those rare and extremely trusting and naive (I won't call them stupid) kids who continued to believe when your contemporaries didn't. If you brought any of your questions to the light for an adult to answer you were met with one of two responses. They either had to admit the sad fact that they were lying to you for years or they repeated the "please just suspend your disbelief and embrace the wonder" mantra of all those Santa Claus movies. You know, the ones that either gave some lame excuse for Santa's ability to live outside the laws of time and space or made you feel like a total scrooge if you didn't just believe the magic. Because we want to believe the magic. If life was just an endless cycle of getting up, eating, working, and going back to sleep until we die then we are facing some serious depression. And we need a lot of drugging, in one form or another, to numb that pointless existence.

You see, we all have that seed of faith in our hearts. We want to believe in something bigger than ourselves. We know, down deep in our subconscious, that God exists. Because without the magic, life is pointless. And God is the one who put that need for meaning there. He is helping us find him. The Santa Claus story and all the other super hero stories we dream up are just a pale copy of the story of who God is. He is omniscient; knowing everything at once, both past and future. He is omnipresent; everywhere and with everyone at once. If we have to accept his love by faith then let your faith stretch even further out to accept his nature. It's like magic, kids.

I think of it this way. God created us with a piece of

himself implanted in everyone. That part of himself goes with us throughout our lives, never leaving us or forsaking us. I have my own part of God's big giant heart that is for me alone. And that part is always available, in fact always waiting and hoping to be with me. And my piece is the same as the whole, so I don't have a pint-sized version of God or just a slice of the cake. I have the whole cake and can eat it too. And I often think of the parts of him that are with someone who is really, really trapped in sin, maybe a murderer or a sex offender. He still spends all his time with that person, wounded by the sin and calling out to them, wanting nothing more than to save them from themselves, and to keep them from hurting others. But I can make God happy by being with him, by choosing him and listening to him. Do you get that? Instead of bringing him grief and leaving him with longing and heartache I can bring joy to the God of the Universe. For he is my God too.

Would you please consider bringing your piece of God joy also? The more joy we bring him the brighter we shine, and the more the darkness flees. Let's push back

the darkness together.

Now that's something to live for.

Just because we choose to accept something by faith doesn't mean we leave all logic and reason behind. God gave us our minds and he expects us to use them. Just like sometimes I have seen people healed miraculously by the hand of God and sometimes they are healed with the use of medicines and the knowledge man has accumulated. I still say God is the one who heals because the intelligence that thought up those medicines and techniques was made by him in the first place. And the Bible itself is really like a giant word puzzle, full of symbolism, logical arguments, translation puzzles, and poetry. There's enough in there to keep an active, questing intellect satisfied for years. The decision itself to choose to believe is a conscious decision, routed in the logical assumption that to believe is better than to not believe.

But after the choosing, which we need to do on a daily, sometimes hourly basis, the ability to act on the choosing can only come out of love. And that love has to come from HIM. Therefore time must be spent with HIM acquiring that love, so we can give it back. That's logical, isn't it?

I have some friends who decided at one point in their attempt to know Jesus more that the answer was found in following the law (rules) of the Old Testament. This seemed like a terrible idea to me, mostly because, as I've established, I hate following rules. But I did try to listen to them with an open mind. I know that I don't know everything, even if the thought of having to give up ham and not being able to bake a cake on Saturday gave me the cold shivers.

But I found that a true study of the scriptures does not support this idea. In fact, just the opposite. The Bible, as I read it, clearly states that the purpose of the law was not to help us know him better, though it can do that if you enjoy studying it's intricacies. And it was not designed to make us holy, because it can't. Even the High Priest, after going through an elaborate cleansing ritual, had to have a rope tied around his foot so that when he went into the holy of holies to try to approach God he could be pulled out if God struck him dead. What the law, and all of our striving, is unable to do, Jesus did on the cross. That's why the law was written. Its purpose is to show us that we need a savior. And to say we should try and please him by observing rules that he died to save us from is not only ludicrous but actually a rejection of what he has done. Did he not die hard enough so that we must make up some of it ourselves? Perish the thought! When Jesus said, "It is finished," he meant it. No more striving or offerings needed. **It is finished.**

I loved this realization when it came to me. And I wondered why anyone would reject this simple and freeing message of grace. Then I realized that, in order to receive this grace, you have to trust him completely, like a child trusts that his parents will make supper at the end of the day. Without that child-like trust, it feels much safer to rely on our own ability to make supper. Especially if we have a recipe to follow. Following the "recipe" set out in the Old

Testament law, or any form of religious rules or rituals, may appear to be harder and more holy, but it is actually easier than laying down your life in trust. Because when Jesus fulfilled the requirements of the law for us by pouring out his life, his offering calls for a response. And when we respond to that love, we need to give our all, trusting that he will take care of us. That can be frightening.

But if the only interaction you had with your best friend or marriage partner was to fulfill a list of requirements, would that satisfy you? If so, you should probably seek counseling, because that's not normal. Maybe for a business contract, but not for a true relationship. A relationship requires intimate vulnerability on the part of both parties. Just following rules is not a relationship.

And it is not the proper response to an act of love. Jesus died for love, not to fulfill a contract. If dotting the i's and crossing the t's was all that was needed then he wouldn't have had to suffer so much agony. Remember why he made us. He doesn't want robots who just follow their programming, or slaves who fulfill their duty. He loves us, and wants to be loved back. Unconditionally. Accepting the love and grace of God is the ultimate freedom, but with it comes the ultimate constraint. We give ourselves to the one who gave his life for us. Our love keeps us in check, not rules.

But we can't lay down our lives in love to someone we don't trust, and we can't trust someone we don't know. So it all circles back to building that relationship. It is the key to knowing him, hearing his voice, and having an amazing, purpose-filled life of love.

It is what we have been missing.

And it requires stillness.

CHAPTER EIGHT

"He was despised and rejected by mankind, a man of suffering, and familiar with pain. Like one from whom people hide their faces he was despised, and we held him in low esteem. Surely he took up our pain and bore our suffering, yet we considered him punished by God, stricken by him, and afflicted. But he was pierced for our transgressions, he was crushed for our iniquities; the punishment that brought us peace was on him, and by his wounds we are healed. We all, like sheep, have gone astray, each of us has turned to our own way; and the Lord has laid on him the iniquity of us all."
Isaiah 53:3-6

I have a theory that most people who claim to be atheists are really just mad at God. Something bad happened to them or their life is not going how they would like it so they decide, usually without even realizing it, that they are going to punish God by disowning him. The terrible thing about this idea is that it actually works. God is hurt when those he created to be his companions spit in his face. We were all created to be his family, and when we choose instead to go it alone in the cold, cruel world we feel the emptiness deep in our bones. That is why man has worshiped *something* for all of his existence. Even when our mighty God-given brains conjure up a scientific-sounding reason for our existence, the emptiness remains. So we fill the void with an endless stream of hobbies and pleasures, bowing down at the feet of the God of self. We were made for God, and anything else will never really fulfill us for long. To resist that idea because you don't like your life is not only childish, but ultimately futile.

Remember that I mentioned previously how I was

having an argument with someone who was lamenting about how God wasn't doing anything for him. If you knew how he was raised you'd think he would know better, but it's an emotional response to pain and not one of reasoning, and I have been guilty of it too. It's so easy for us to blame God for what he's supposedly not doing and never give him credit for the good things he has done. I told this person that his dying for us was enough. Even if he never did another thing for you, he gave his life for you when you didn't deserve it. What more does he have to do? Care about your every small need?

Done.

Watch over you at all times and never desert you even when you turn your back and deny him?

Check.

Send his angels to fight for you against the realms of darkness?

Yep.

Give you a world as a giant, beautiful playground

and a mind to create your own objects of beauty and things to help you live an easier life?

That too.

It's all him, people. It's time we stopped whining about the things he supposedly hasn't done for us and start taking stock of what he has done. And he didn't have to do any of it. He could have decided that this whole people project was a wash and given up. But he didn't. You should be glad.

My aunt tells the story about how once when she was having a difficult time she went to McDonalds for a fish sandwich. Now she happened to like sweet and sour sauce on her fish sandwiches. And of course we all know that's a little weird. No normal McDonalds cashier would think to offer sweet and sour sauce with a fish sandwich. And she was feeling so bad about herself that she didn't want to ask. But strange as it may sound, the cashier told her he happened to have some sweet and sour packets in his hand, and did she want them?

That should make you tear up a bit. Because that was her Father God, caring about the little things, just trying to cheer her up. I'm sure there were things that happened in your life (maybe a little less strange) that seemed like lucky breaks or coincidence. But those things were really God loving you.

It's time to try the five minute challenge again. But this time I will make it a bit easier. Instead of having to just be still, I will give us (I haven't let myself off the hook, we are in it together) a task to perform. Let's spend these next five minutes thinking of the things God has done for us, and thanking him. And if you run out of things before you run out of time, start looking around you. Just studying nature alone should give you fodder for several hours of praise. But start with your own life. I am thanking him for you right now. Really. I'm glad you're reading this and still holding my hand.

And on an important side note: please don't think I am trying to minimize any suffering you have gone through. He was there when you were hurt. He went through it with you. He felt it at the cross. And he was not indifferent or too busy or not caring enough to stop what happened. All I can say is that when he made us, he gave us his own will, which is free to choose. He wanted companions, not robotic slaves. So people are free to make bad choices, and sometimes those choices hurt others. But he can and will heal those things if you are willing to bring them to him. But it will take time. Another good reason for five more minutes.

How did it go? I hope it went well for you, that you feel renewed and closer to your God. If not, don't despair. Trust me, he is worth multiple attempts. In fact, it should become part of your daily life. But before you start to panic, just remember that he is always with you, in every bus ride and traffic crawl and session with a sink full of dishes. And he is infinitely patient.

I did my five minutes in the bathtub. For me, that seems to be the place that works best. I think it's because I can't be interrupted easily, like I could if I was just sitting in my bedroom. And I don't just mean by my kids. They are older now and no longer hanging on my legs or wanting my time as much. The real culprit may surprise you. It's not my neighbors, my pets, or even my husband. It's me. I am my own worst enemy when it comes to trying to be still. I am a do-er. A get-er-done-er. I feel good only when I have accomplished something. I feel guilty just sitting around doing nothing, as if it was a vacation I haven't earned. And sitting and just being with God seems like doing nothing.

Because being open and intimate with God is not bringing him a laundry list of prayer needs. I can do that without guilt, because then I am accomplishing something, and it is usually not for myself. Of course there is a time for that, but it is not what I am talking about here. I hope I have been clear on that. If you want to have a meaningful interaction with your spouse you don't just sit and read off a list of stuff you want them to do and then rush off before they can even answer you. Even a time of prayer should actually be better than that, but that's for another book. This is about you and God getting close, about you knowing him so well that you can hear his voice at any time, and have confidence in who you are as his child.

This skill is vital. Absolutely essential. It is actually not a waste of time, or a vacation from real work, but it is THE most important thing you could ever do with your time. Better than saving little Timmy from the well and doing open-heart surgery on him at the same time. It is building the skill that *tells* you little Timmy is in the well and *gives* you the confidence and wisdom to fix his broken heart. Think of it as you signing up to serve in God's ranks. He is your general. You have your field manual, the Bible, which can help guide you when you are out of touch with headquarters. But if you are suddenly in the thick of battle you need not only the ability to make an instant life or death decision, but also the confidence in yourself and your training to carry out that decision. Knowing your general, and getting trained by him personally, could be the difference between life and death. And not just for you, but for those around you.

Don't think I am exaggerating. This life is a battle. If you haven't figured that out yet you are pretty naive, and I am about to burst your happy little bubble. Just think back to your attempts in the five minute challenges. Why was it so hard? Looking at it logically, it shouldn't have been. You have control over your own mind, don't you? You are probably an adult, or close to it, and can keep still in a chair for five minutes, can't you?

94

You see, we have an enemy. Even if you are not a Christian and haven't enlisted in God's army, he is still your enemy. There is no getting away from it. Satan hates us all. Not because we are so hate-worthy, but because he hates God. And hurting God's people, destroying his creation, is what the devil lives for. He has nothing else, because he has already been defeated. So be prepared to do battle. Stir up the warrior inside you and put on your big boy pants. And remember, your savior Jesus who loves you died to make your victory possible. So, as my pastor would say, we fight *from* the win, not *for* it. Do you understand that? It means we can fight with the assurance that we will win. We have already won! There is no need for fear of failure, no need for anxiety and what ifs. Have the confidence that Jesus bought for you.

And when you get weary, he will give you rest. Even in the midst of the fight. But it's your job to know him so you can understand how to find that rest.

It starts in five minutes.

Let's go again. And yes, I mean right away. You don't have another five minutes you say? You must be an important person. I should apologize for having bothered you. But unless you have to perform life saving surgery or jump out of an airplane or defuse a bomb I am going to call you a liar. You're pants are *so* on fire.

How about I **really** hold your hand through this one? You can come along with me and see how it goes for the know-it-all writing this book. I promise to be real.

I am setting a timer.

Minute one: "Hi God. I really didn't want to write today. I haven't written in awhile and it is hard to get going. I feel like a failure. And I know you would tell me that I am not, and that every day is a new day, but it's hard today. I want to escape. And I am terrified of failing the people who are reading it. You know how badly I want to help people. I don't want them to have to flail around like I did."

Minute two: "I'm just gonna take a few deep breaths. I will allow your peace to fill me. I will choose to trust in you." I breathe.

Minute three: "I know you've got this, Jesus. You want to help them more than I do. You put that desire to help inside me. You are everything good in my life. You are my inspiration. I love you Lord. I really love you."

Minute four: I think about his love. I let it soak in. Then my mind wanders and I feel guilty.

Minute five: I think the time is almost up. I check the timer. Yep, just one minute more. But it's not enough. I need more of him. More peace. More assurance. I feel a momentary panic at having to go back to life. But I will choose to be faithful and go back to writing. I tell myself I will find more time later to talk to him. I will practice remembering he is always with me.

Now we're done. Of course they don't always go like that. And now, when I should have loads of inspirational stuff to write about, I still find myself dry and empty. But I do feel at peace. And I know he is with me, and I can talk to him at any time. And I want him to help me find more minutes in my day, so I can keep filling up my bucket of peace. I know there is a hole in the bottom, and it trickles out as the day goes on. But he designed it that way. If I could get all I needed in one five minute session then I wouldn't need to have much of a relationship at all. Imagine spending only five minutes a day with your spouse, or your kids, or your best friend or even your boss. You would be like strangers on the bus, chatting about the weather and never developing any deep connection. God wants more from you. And it is there, in the relationship, that you learn what he is like, how much he loves you, and how to tap into that love to carry you through life.

And see, I did have something to say after all.

I sincerely pray that it helps you.

CHAPTER NINE

"You make known to me the path of life; you will fill me with joy in your presence, with eternal pleasures at your right hand."
Psalm 16:11

I remember once I watched a documentary about a group of missionaries who traveled to a remote region in a jungle somewhere. It was a very moving story. The natives were desperate to know what happened after their loved ones died. I think they had a legend in their culture that said if they sent out an inquiry in a certain form over the water then some mysterious force might answer. I don't remember what exactly they did, but I believe they sent out a raft, Gilligan's Island style, and just hoped for an answer. And God heard their cry and sent some missionaries. Pretty cool, right? God saw them and heard their desperation. That's the kind of God he is.

But that was not the most memorable part of the story, at least to me. What struck me most was how the missionaries approached the idea of giving the people their answer. They started a Bible school and began teaching it from the beginning, starting with creation and not revealing the idea of salvation coming by the cross right away. I understand why they did this. They didn't want the people to misunderstand or misinterpret things or just plain get weird. And I know from other stories I read about, that this can happen. Enthusiastic people who were given just a portion of scripture did some weird things because they didn't get the whole story.

But I still think those missionaries were wrong. I know, who do I think I am? I'm just a nobody from small town Wisconsin and I dare criticize people who gave up their lives (not to mention their flushing toilets) to help people know the good news of salvation? Yes, I am a nobody, and yes, I greatly admire people who travel far from home and endure hardships to preach the gospel. The greatest hardship I am facing right now is a backache from an uncomfortable chair. I am not criticizing missionaries. I am making a point. If someone is hungry should we give them a sandwich or take them to a restaurant and show them how it is made? If someone is cold do we give them a coat or take them on a tour of the coat factory?

The most heartbreaking part of the story to me was

when one of the older natives was dying and they sent for the missionaries and begged them to give him the answer so he wouldn't have to die in ignorance and fear. Of course I am pretty sure they told him. Otherwise I think I would have thrown something through the television. But how long did he lie there wondering? How long had they left him to linger in fear when they had the antidote in their hands? It seemed cruel to me. Maybe those people never got weird, but I'm not sure it was worth it.

It is important that we know the Bible and understand the whole story. But these people had waited years for the answer to their desperate question. Instead of just saying, yes, death is not the end, and yes, someone loves you enough to make a way for you to live forever and also live a full meaningful life on earth, they withheld that joy. They put them in school. They made them earn the right to know the answer. That is not what Jesus did when he was here on earth. We are not to be like the religious leaders of his day that he criticized so openly and harshly.

He said they loaded down people's backs with heavy demands and restrictions and didn't lift one finger to help move them.

I don't want to do that to you. That is why this book has been blunt and not filled with flowery text and awe-inspiring Bible knowledge. I want you to know without a doubt that Jesus loves you. That God wants you. Needs you. Longs for you. Desires to spend time with you. Wants to teach you himself. Forgives you, grieves over you, weeps for you.

Please read the Bible. Watch sermons on Youtube. Attend a church. Don't get weird. But mostly, don't wait to know him. Don't think you have to pass some sort of test to speak with him, or hear his voice. Jesus paid your tuition and more when he died for you. All you have to do is choose him, and show up. Don't wait. I know you're hungry now.

And I brought a sandwich.

There will come a day, if it hasn't already, when you feel nothing. No desire to seek God but also no fear or anger towards him. Just nothing. Everyone has those days, when you're just going through the motions of life. It's really a form of mild depression. You could try a little exercise or some extra sunlight on your face, and while you're there spend some time with God anyway. Remember he already knows how you feel, so you don't need to apologize for feeling blah. You aren't disappointing him. In fact, just because you chose to be with him when you didn't feel like it pleases him immensely. I hope I haven't been too repetitive on this point but it's extremely important to get it right. Don't let *your* feelings dictate how God feels about you. He loves you no matter what.

But now that you've chosen him that doesn't necessarily mean your apathetic feelings have gone away. Sometimes the act of choosing is enough to bring the sun back out but other times the blahs are just too strong. That's when you could use a little outside help. There are a number of good devotionals out there, and I will put a list of my favorites at the end of this book. But I am here to help you right now. Remember we are doing this together.

I am a homeschool mom so I have done a fair amount of writing classes over the years. Usually I am too cheap to buy a lot of pre-packaged curriculum so I just do some research on what's out there and try to re-create it myself using something that I have on hand, or my own imagination. I know you are not very impressed with me right now but my kids have turned out okay so far. But one book that always intrigued me was called "Story Starters". It was basically a book where the beginning of the story was written for you, to help give you a jump if you couldn't come up with a good idea or had writer's block. I never purchased that book (cheap, remember) but I think the idea would work out for us now. I will call them "Five Minute Starters", and you can use them on the blah days or when you feel like you need a little help getting started talking to God.

And don't think too highly of me for coming up with them. I will just use my own experience, and I have had a lot. That's a nicer way of saying I am old.

Here's the first one:

Read Philippians 2:13. Write it down. Memorize it. Now go to God and start your time by saying it aloud and claiming it yourself. This is my example, and you can just quote me if you want. But acknowledge in your heart that it is *you* saying these things, and agreeing with them. You are just using my words.

"Father God, your word says that you would do the work for me. I need you to do that. I don't have the ability, or even the desire to want the ability today. But you promised in this verse that you would give me the will to do it and the ability to act on it. I claim this for me. Make it so. Take me out of the doldrums and be the wind in my sail today. I want to feel something. I want to be at peace, to have joy, even to feel sorrow if it will bring healing to my heart. Remove this sloth from my soul. Show me you are real, and that you keep your promises."

    Amen.

When I was pregnant with my second child I became very depressed. I had morning sickness all day and a three-year-old to take care of. I had been sick with the first one too, and had high hopes that it wouldn't be as bad the second time around. In all reality, I had hopes that there would never *be* a second time around. The adventure of marriage and child-rearing had faded, and the thought of another one would only mean I would be stuck at home longer. I had dreams, and they didn't include cleaning toilets and wiping noses for the rest of the foreseeable future. I felt like I was worth nothing, and had nothing to look forward too, and that this was somehow my punishment for getting pregnant with my first child before I was married. Hence the depression.

I did warn you I would be real.

Someone, I don't remember exactly who it was, but I think it was a friend of my Mom's, told me she had a "word" for me. I knew that my Mom had a group of praying friends and of course I was touched, yet a little leery of so-called "words from God" from someone I didn't know well. But I was also desperate. It was a simple scripture verse, but being told that it was for me specifically from God made it very personal, and not just some Bible story. I wrote it down and taped it up on my kitchen cupboard where I would see it every day. I read the story it came out of. And I pondered it.

Basically I just thought about it a lot.

It took awhile, but the meaning gradually sunk into my hard heart and it has become my favorite verse to this day. Now I will share it with you and pray that if it is something you need to hear then The Holy Spirit will help it sink into your heart as well.

Read Acts 10: 1-35. The specific verse that was given to me is verse 15.

Read the highlighted verse again.

Now let's go before God. "Father, you say here in your word that if I have been cleansed by you, and I have through the blood of your son, then I am clean. And to entertain the notion that I am not, or to listen to accusations that say I am not, or to agree with anyone, even my own thoughts, that say I am not, **is wrong.** In fact, it is a *command* that I not call myself impure. You commanded Peter to not say such a thing, even though the opposite command was written in the law. We think it is a good and noble thing to put ourselves down, or wallow in our sinfulness. But Jesus died for the pagan centurion, and he died for me, to make us clean. Everything changed when he died, and to agree with something else is to spit on his bleeding face. I will not do that. I am clean. Jesus Christ has made me clean. I will not believe anything else. Ever."

You could write that verse down and put it up somewhere you can see it everyday too.

I have it on my bathroom mirror right now.

CHAPTER TEN

"Do not gloat over me, my enemy! Though I have fallen, I will rise. Though I sit in darkness, the Lord will be my light."
Micah 7:8

The women in my family had a movie night recently. We watched yet another cinematic version of Louisa May Alcott's classic novel "Little Women". I have read the book (and many others by the same author) and liked it. But my daughter commented that she was surprised that I liked the story. She said it was both too sad and too preachy to be something I would normally go for. And I thought about it for awhile and realized that she was right. The main reason I liked the book was because I saw myself as being a lot like one of the main characters. Joe March is me in many ways. She saw the world as being too restrictive for a girl, and wished she had been a boy. She was not as beautiful as her other three sisters. She enjoyed writing. She did not have a problem befriending a boy. She questioned things, and struggled with the idea that she could improve herself. I could've been describing myself there. One major difference between us, other than the fact that she is a fictional character, is that she was able to reconcile herself to the whole self-improvement thing. I never have.

And I never will.

The idea is absurd. It is purely wishful thinking. I'm not saying it's wrong to try to be good, or to seek to improve your mind or have goals or anything like that. I am only saying that the philosophy of believing a person can, by sheer force of will, somehow better themselves is a load of do-do. And do-do is not the word I am thinking of. And it's downright criminal to teach people that they can do it. What happens when they eventually fail? Do you tell them to try harder? Do you imply that they must not have wanted it enough? I can tell you that the despair that can result from that is not something fun to live with. It is why many people choose not to try again, or commit suicide when they can't keep "dusting themselves off".

You may find this a strong opinion. You may be right. You may think *I* am full of do-do. But please trust my experience. Improving yourself, or conquering your own sins, **will not work**. Not in the long run. You may succeed for a short while, and some very strong-willed people or those with a lot of self-discipline can make it seem to work, but it never truly lasts.

We are born with a selfish nature. And our selfishness causes us to not want to improve ourselves in any way that might actually hurt ourselves. We protect ourselves always. If you don't believe this you are either very naive or very self-deceived, or both. Ever wonder why nobody had to teach us how to fight? Or how to look after our own interests? Comes natural, doesn't it? Nobody has to train a two-year-old to fight for a toy. We were born thinking we are the center of the universe, but without the ability to take ourselves off center stage. We *can't* make ourselves good.

Galatians 5:17 states "For the flesh desires what is contrary to the Spirit, and the Spirit what is contrary to the flesh. They are in conflict with each other, so that you are not to do whatever you want." Now back up to verse 16. "So I say, walk by the Spirit, and you will not gratify the desires of the flesh." The Spirit referred to here is the Holy

Spirit. The real *good* in us only comes through surrendering our lives to Jesus, and letting him live through us. This is walking in the Spirit.

Jesus gave up his life, even when he knew some of those he was dying for would still reject him. He **was** the center of the universe, but he became a homeless human, subject to hunger and hurt and hangnails. And he **didn't** fight for his rights. He humbled himself, and sacrificed himself, not just so we could go to heaven, but so we could live a better life right now. He gave up a lot to do it. Most of us can't even give up the best slice of cake. So let's not belittle his sacrifice by trying to do it ourselves.

This brings us back to the point of this book. We need to spend time with him, to learn how to walk in the Spirit. Without him in our lives, filling us every day, we keep eating the best piece of cake, even though it sits in our gut like a rock. Do you want something to set your strong will at? Something that will actually be productive? **Spend time with him.** The only way to improve yourself is to let him do it in you. And the only way that happens is when you spend time with him, learning about him and from him. We need to have our selfish heart replaced with his. He was the only person who walked the earth who needed no improvement.

And the cool thing about this is that God *knows* this about us. He is not upset that we can't fix ourselves. He does not expect us to be able to fix ourselves. He wants to be needed remember? So don't feel bad about your weakness, and don't try to make yourself strong. Run to your Daddy's arms and let him make it better.

Read John 15:1-17 and highlight verse 5.

"Jesus, I want to understand what you are saying here. Please help me. I want to bear good fruit. I want to be able to love others. I know I can't by myself. As I read it again, plant the words deep in my heart and keep reminding me all day, every day, whenever I need it. I need to be planted in you directly, not through someone else or some religious program. I need you to flow into me. I want to accept your pruning for my good, and produce even more fruit next time. Help me set my will to being with you every day."

"But the fruit of the Spirit is love, joy, peace, forbearance, kindness, faithfulness, gentleness and self control." (Galatians 5:22&23)

Today I needed comfort. I was feeling bad about myself. I had a bad week. I imagine you have had those too. How do you handle it? Do you have a drink, eat a pint of ice cream, or cry on someone's shoulder? What if you can't do any of those things? Or you've done them all and they don't alleviate the pain?

It's time for another five minutes.

Actually five minutes won't be enough.

Here's what happened. It's going to sound stupid. And petty. And I assure you I have experienced tragedy and heartbreak and emotional and physical pain that makes this week look like a walk in the park. But I also know that your pain is your pain. There is always something worse that can happen, or something worse that has happened to someone somewhere. That thought doesn't make the pain you feel at that moment go away. And it doesn't mean the pain you have isn't real or worth dealing with. Even the small stuff can break you down. And I was feeling broken down.

I was washing the dishes and I was tired. I was physical tired and emotionally tired. I felt like everyone around me got to do fun things and I was stuck in a rut of drudgery. No one appreciated the things I did. And no one cared enough about me to try to help me. I was forgotten.

Unattractive.

Unloved.

I told you it was stupid. But when I started crying into my dishwater I knew something was wrong and I knew what I needed. I needed some God time.

I hadn't spent time alone with him all day, and not much time the previous day either. It had been a busy time and I didn't make time with him a priority. I was paying for it now. But it was fixable.

I took a bath and poured out my heart to my savior. I cried. I vented. I sat and was still. Then, after awhile, I heard him speak to me. And I received the comfort I needed. I know many of you reading this don't hear his voice like I do. And that's fixable too. It just takes practice, like anything else.

In junior high I played the drums. For about nine months. I liked the drums. I could make myself practice most of the time. But as soon as I learned that I would have to go back to school every week during the summer to practice with my teacher, I quit. Going back into that hated building and spending any amount of *my* summer in school was too much of a sacrifice. It wasn't worth it. So today I cannot play the drums.

Anything worth while is going to take practice. It will take commitment. And you will have to count the cost. But I can say with absolute certainty that sacrificing some of your day to God is worth the cost. In fact, after awhile of practice, if you skip time you will miss it. You will feel the absence of it, like skipping a meal or a shower or a daily hug from the one you love. To go without it will make you feel empty and depressed. But when you start again it will feel like slipping back into your comfortable slippers after being in heels all day. Or snuggling on the couch in a warm blanket on a cold night.

So practice with me. I will share a bit of what God told me while I sat in the tub to give you a taste of what you could have. Hopefully it will be like hearing a talented musician play, and it will encourage you to pick up your own instrument and practice so you too can play like that someday.

"I see you beloved. I love you. You are never unnoticed by me. I saw the little things you did that nobody else noticed. It pleased me. I am pleased by you." Then I tried to argue with God, I told him that I could have done more, that I was selfish and stupid. That the little things mean nothing. He gently interrupted my tirade against myself. "Accept the fact that I am pleased. Do not take away my joy by putting yourself down. I am the one who helped you do those small things, and I don't see anything as small like you do. Those things meant much to me, and you did them. **I am pleased.** Remember that even if you do nothing, I am pleased with you because you are here with me, loving me. That is all I want. Let everything else go, and rest in my pleasure."

So I did. And there are no earthly pleasures that can compare to the pleasure of God.

Trust me.

I have been reading one of my grandmother's journals. It has been enlightening, and rather sad. She was someone I looked up to. I thought she had great faith, and I wanted to be like her. I remember when she was facing death she confided in me that she was afraid to go because she didn't think she had anything worthwhile to give to Jesus when she reached heaven. I was shocked at the time. I thought her whole entire life was a giant offering to God. Reading her journal confirmed that she felt inadequate most of her life. This not only saddened me, it worried me too. If she fell short, what hope was there for someone like me?

Now, don't get confused here. I'm not talking about the ability to gain entrance into heaven. Jesus died to pay the way for that, all we have to do is believe in him. But when you get there, will he say to you "Well done, good and faithful servant?" Will the life you lived before death serve as something that stands before him or will you have to hang your head in shame at the wastefulness of it all?

And I don't mean good works. Many good works are done to make ourselves feel good or look good to others, and those things don't count. God looks at the heart. What was our heart motive? Did we live for him, or ourselves?

Going back to my grandmother, I can say with confidence that her life pleased God. I saw the fruit of it. I lived it. She was the one who believed in me when I was a mess, and made me feel loved regardless, and that was a *huge* thing for me. It meant more than a thousand lectures or sermons. That was her being Jesus to me, when I wasn't sure what I believed. And I know she did that for many people.

So why was she so hard on herself? That's a question I cannot answer. I wish I could. Because, you see, I am like her. I can easily see my short-comings, and I criticize every word I speak and view every action as not being good enough. I feel insecure about this book. Am I being too harsh? Too real? Is it not compelling enough, or does it not meet any real need? Am I just kidding myself that there are others out there like me? I don't know the answers to those questions either. In the world of Facebook fakeness and Instagram instant intelligence am I just an old fashioned fool to lay my heart out on the table like this?

Maybe. But one thing I do know. I don't want to get to the end of my life still feeling inadequate. I don't want to wonder if I am pleasing to God or not. I want to KNOW that I KNOW that I KNOW. You know? I want to be confident in who I am in Christ and who I am in this world. And I want to help others know that too.

So here is my heart on the table for you to dissect. Call me a fool. Say you don't believe in God or in hearing his voice. Tell me that I am leading you down the primrose path and it will break you when God doesn't answer how you want him to. Well, I never said he would. Believing in God and hearing his voice doesn't guarantee a smooth path down life's road. Everyone will have their dark nights of the soul, whether they believe in God or not. I just want to know that someone is there when I do go through the darkness. That someone has my back. And that someone is all-powerful, all-loving, and always present. And I want to be able to hear his voice and feel his hand. I want him to be my adequateness. My more-than-adequateness. I want to count on him so I don't have to count on myself. I want to be real, but I don't want to make anyone sad. I want that to be both what I have to offer Jesus at the pearly gates and what I leave behind as my legacy.

And that's truly an art.

By the way, thanks for holding my hand.

About Me

Up in Wisconsin is where I live,
Homeschooling advice I am happy to give.
And though I despise winter's cruel freeze,
I have enjoyed a lot of great cheese.
Four awesome kids have come out of me;
Of cats I have owned, there have been three.
Gardening and reading I do enjoy,
In board games much luck I can employ.
And while my hubby works for a living wage,
I get to chase characters around the page.
(Thanks beloved)

Please consider leaving a review on Amazon and as many stars as you think this book deserves. If you liked it, help spread the word on social media and hopefully others can start holding my hand too. Thanks for reading!

Suggestions For Further Reading
Or
Other stuff I liked.

Jesus Calling and/or Jesus Today by Sarah Young
Grace For The Moment by Max Lucado
And I Will Be found By You by Francis Frangipane
Adventures in Prayer by Catherine Marshall
Hungry for More of Jesus by David Wilkerson

You can also visit my author page on Amazon for more
books by me.